ISOLATOR

ISOLATOR

MONICA CARROLL

RECENT
WORK
PRESS

Isolator
Recent Work Press
Canberra, Australia

Copyright © Monica Carroll 2017

National Library of Australia
Cataloguing-in-Publication entry is available at
http://catalogue.nla.gov.au.
ISBN: 9780648087830 (paperback)

All rights reserved. This book is copyright. Except for private study, research, criticism or reviews as permitted under the Copyright Act, no part of this book may be reproduced, stored in a retrieval system, or transmitted in any form by any means without prior written permission. Enquiries should be addressed to the publisher.

Cover image: Trench Mask, Ian Livesey
Cover design: Recent Work Press
Set by: Recent Work Press

recentworkpress.com

I listen to the speaking of the wire.

It tells me you should piss off and not read this.

But you're a nosey little bugger

aren't you?

HUGO

Hey dude.

I like it here. My northern window is catching a breeze and a pup is sleeping in a sun patch near my bed. There's red dust on everything, and I've got a durrie in the ashtray. Couldn't ask for anything more. This is the fairest life.

I wrote a letter to Kyle and sent it. I was feeling pretty ballsy. Bit different with the Station Hands though. Whenever I'm around them I get butter-fingers and go shy. I don't much like them so it must be your influence that makes me act up wild.

I am giving my all here. The work is not easy but I want to save up for a car. I got to drive a pre-historic Holden in the dust. She was hard to steer so I was fishtailing everywhere. Brian kept up saying, 'Slow down, woman', while the kids kept up saying, 'Faster, Hannah, faster'. Deep down, I'm a hoon for sure.

Working the radio is tops. 'This is Romeo Sierra calling S.O.T.A. Come in, over.' 'We hear you faintly, are you on channel 5145 or 5845?' Sounds a bit flash, I know.

My training course in Port Pirie was a rage. I got pissed with a bunch of other governesses. I played it straight and didn't be a sleaze. I'm sworn off men—they are TROUBLE. (Don't hold me to that.)

We're out of school Hu—no-one but us to blame for life now.

Write soon. Miss you.
Hannah

Under the bed.
Come on down here with me.
Crawl under.

I burrowed through the arse of this book, looking for you

    I had to eat the pages.

The hollow came over him, as it often did before seeing though a commitment beyond the threshold. Instead of meeting with his Go group, he hides in bed with a sore throat and an almost certain oncoming flu. The body is handmaiden to wild fear.

What would his mother have said?

"If you want people to like you, be nice to them."

'*Nice*', on this page, means:

(a) let yourself be ill-treated and harmed
(b) forget the protective boundaries around your body
(c) give up whatever it takes to be liked because:

    i. being liked is more important than feeling safe
    ii. you're worthless so if someone talks to you, be grateful
    iii. show your gratitude by never saying 'No' because:

        1. people won't like you if you say 'No'
        2. you're not allowed to say 'No'
        3. If you say 'No', they will:

            a.   Bash you
            b.   Rape you
            c.   Molest you
            d.   Stab you
            e.   Laugh at you
            f.   Spit on you
            g.   Chase you
            h.   Leave you

If you want to say 'No', be quiet instead.

Righto, let me do something fancy for you. This is a book, after all.

Tick all that apply

"Come here. I've got a stretch of

☐ thick black plastic
☐ wet earth
☐ leather soaked in chloroform
☐ aggressive imagination

for you."

Tick one, you bastard! No one gets off lightly. No free rides. It's not a peep show. It's a book.

Commit.

HUGO

How's life dude?

Ta for the long letter! Your job in the bin sounds grand; a mop to call your own. Too bad they don't pay you.

I had a great night at the Roxby Downs pub. I'm busting to tell you about the most flawless hunk who learned me up on things to do in the Downs after dark; like sneaking into the library at 4am, and stealing a mining ute with an explosives trunk on the tray. Christ, I had huge fun and I didn't even fuck him. I fooled about but it wasn't dirty. Forgive me, Hu, but he had the BIGGEST COCK I've ever grabbed. Oh. He was a tight package with messy hair and dusty jeans. Hell, I was done for. I reckon even you would have wanted a poke, Hu.

Ahem. Well, back to reality.

I avoided Leon after that as I couldn't rub the grin off my mug.

You're lucky you don't have to vote. I do.

Station Life is all the usual:

Brian browbeats me, Everything is scorched, I am filthy dirty, Everything blisters, Work tests me, I kill 300 insects a day, Every fucking thing is ablaze, All I do is sweat.

My house is a total tip—slob is my destiny.

Write soon. Miss you.
Hannah

He wonders why he is not dead.

In a book there is a story about a famous poet who once told a younger poet she was not allowed to use the word 'spirit' in her poem.

"You have not *earned* the right."

She stabbed him then wrote a poem in his honour.

> *Spirit spirit spirit spirit*
>
> *Spirit spirit spirit*
>
> *Spirity spirit o' spirit spirit spirit*

When you cannot go *Out There* you find ways to make it sensible *In Here*.

You create coherence for yourself which is, categorically, a type of madness.

For the longest time—if time were a knitted jumper hanging well past the knees—his concern for going* insane was concealed in tins, jars, and fruit with a thick peel.

⋆as if to a destination, such as Hawaii

Experience taught him,

    1. Madness is but just a moment

    2. You can convince some of the people
                                            some of the time

    3. The Sanatorium is unsanitary

Can you hear the wire? It talky talks to you.

You read too easily.

Look underneath the ink. Scratch it away.

Speak the hidden.

HU!

Thanks for the choice letter.

How are you?!?
Sounds like you are having a totally excellent time as a cuckoo coconut. You looney toon extraordinaire.

This will be a Letter In Disarray because I have a mammoth hangover and the DTs make it hard to have dominion over this fucking pen.

Christ, I feel crook. My house is a tragedy. If Sonya sees it she will freak but I am too ill to clean it up.

Roxby last night I,
(i) sliced my leg open after I fell on a pint glass
(ii) dirty-danced with a mullet on the table
(iii) sculled many inebriating beverages
(iv) had a slick time with the boys drinking & playing cards.

We're sleeping out tonight. Bazillions of sheep get loaded onto cattle trucks after midnight. Won't that be a joy? I'm into the camping so long as they don't pitch my tent at the far end of the paddock. Away from the boys. They would prefer it if I 'ceased associations'. Hell, they're just friends.

I'm gonna make you a tape of my moaning from this hangover. Double-sided 90.

If it was the old days in Canberra I'd shuffle to your house and say, 'Hey Hugo, I feel dog-awful'. You'd say, 'So do I'. We'd nurse our throbbing heads and stare at our hands shaking like timber. We'd fry a major breakfast and watch TV all day.

Hugo—I have put on weight so bad. My maroon pants, the ones I used to wear all the time—I can't get them on. I'm devastated. What am I going to do?

By the way, our pet calf died. Bless her little cow spirit.

See ya later

Hannah
xxx

ISOLATING BEHAVIOURS

☐ Dressing like a banana
☐ Saying yes to social functions
         then not attending
☐ Displaying diseases
☐ Kissing your pentagram for 'luck'
☐ Talking too much
☐ Displaying knowledge
☐ Punching them in the face

HUG

The sun is shining and the day is a beauty.

Rain last night. The world is mud. Dogs and lambs are frolicking together. Cats are asleep on the bonnet of the roo-shooter's trucks. The drone of the shooters' bikes surrounds my house. It reminds me of a lazy Sunday at home, listening to the lawnmowers.

Yesterday, Ace and Max got me on a motorbike—it was so much fun. I love going fast! Can't wait to get back on the thing.

Leon is in Adelaide, on holiday. I miss him. He is cuddly and always holds my hand. He held my hand for all of the Roxby trip. He even did it in front of his mates and it didn't bother him. In fact, he liked it.

We shared a room in Roxby. I told him I wasn't on anything. I expected him to whip out a packet of frangers. I'd decided to do it with him, if I had to, so I could keep him. He said, 'I didn't expect you to do anything.' I know Hu, I'm a moron.

We lay in bed eating Fantales & watching Rage. I didn't know any of the songs. What a yokel. We had a shower and washed each other's back and cracks.

What do you make of him, Hu? I reckon you'd get on with him as if you'd known him all your life. He's an A-rad boyfriend.

Write soon

Hannah

Nothing touching

the first cobblestone on the road to alone

Nothing touching

Buttons on a cuff, when in
pairs, must be tailored down to one.

Large dining tables of beaten
oak are furnished with a single chair.

    Where there is a saucer there must be no cup.

Isolation is a state of pleasing discordance. Nothing must. Not needs. Not want. It is a state of below-belly desire—not groinal, nor lustful, but where the world smacks into the mind of its own.

Sometimes that means fucking. Other times being fucked. Nothing must fit. The ground is uneven and stirs underfoot. When love is found it can be lavished upon with lies and flattery. Then forgotten.

Isolation is a pattern. It is life as calm discomfort.
Fucking, being fucked.

HUGO

Just writing to let you know I'm still alive!

So much to tell you when I come home. Make sure you're out.

I shot a rifle—thought I'd be crap but I hit the target first shot. (Poor beer can.)

Work never quits. If I'm not in the schoolroom, I'm washing fucking dishes. But I'll go to Marla this weekend if the rain doesn't stuff up the roads. I need a break.

Hugo—I'm homesick. Been here for near 10 months and only been homesick for a week. But this is a bad case. Miss you, love you.

See ya soon

Han

This is the part that harks back to your childhood encounter of being alone and hidden from those around you. Tucked behind a curtain, curled in a cupboard. Laid out like a lolly under that bed.

Write your memory here:

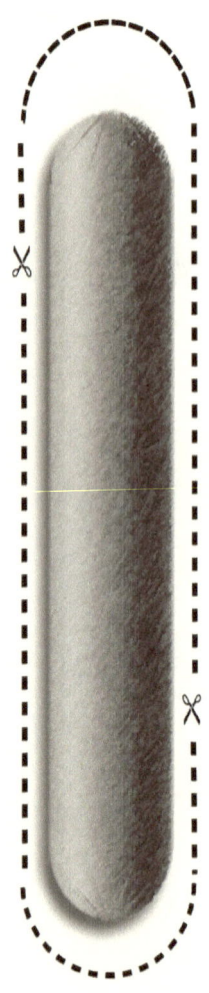

If life demands you use a hot dog &
you find yourself with none to hand,
grasp this.

Use this page to wrap your hot dog

Use this page to wrap your hot dog

Dear Hugo

I can't post this until Sonya orders stamps. Might be a while as she's a tetchy old cow.

Smoking: I've cut back to six a day. This is mega. How do I achieve this magical feat? Well, I'm glad you asked. I smoke half a fag then put it out. An hour later I have the other half.

Leon: reckons I have the irrits with him. This is good.

Leon II: Done. I told him it was off. The room went werid, Hu. I was all calm and scientific. He cried. I feel awful for him, but what is done is right. I am getting on with my life. I'm better off single. Truthfully, I'm hopeless at being faithful.

Oh, Hu, do you know how it feels to break a guy's heart? He was devastated.

Work: Tops. The kids are schooling hard. Sonya tries to treat me better.

Sketches: Well, Kylie sprayed her dog, Quik, with perfume and now she is all sticky and she stinks.

'Beast', Ace's dingo-x-collie, attacked Sonya's sister's dog, 'Priscilla', and bit a chunk from its shoulder. It's a prissy mutt. Sonya's sister feeds P grilled chops & all the best meat off her plate.

Station: Electricity problems again. Lamb-tailing's started at Mt Eba. Work overload for everyone.

Why did I set this letter out with headings? Stupid isn't it?
Write soon.
Your Hannah

If the object is to family oneself with corruption—and I mean this in the moral sense—the choices are infinite. You can dress your children in bruises. Or play grown-up feely games with their child parts. Record your grooming. Confine them. Stuff them. Starve them. Watch them lie for you. Watch them bleed. Use plain old blackmail—the black kind—if you're a tad weary. Try to wreck them while you have the chance. Family is the polite word for hostage.

We all have to do them—
        have them done on us.

Hugo.

Wow!!

Your letter was totally amazing. I can't believe no-one checks the showers after 10pm.

Have you had Rob yet? Is he good?! I must admit, he sounds like a nice-looker. And don't you dare squander Rob's rock-harder. You know how I feel about wasting nature's little wonders.

Anyway, as Leon is no longer my little man, I had a peek to see what Ace was made of. (Yep. Mega-sleaze; make myself puke.) I snuck him into my room (tsk tsk) and fooled around all Saturday night. We didn't do it but I feasted on him. Oh man, this dude is beautiful, Hu. I felt like I was going to melt, or explode, or turn inside out. Do you get what I'm trying to say? I've had a rather dry spell for 6 months, sure, but maybe it's just Ace. What do you think?

He told me how he dreamt I was totally covered in tinned pineapple and he ate his way to me. Funny as; especially as we hold tinned pineapple in such high esteem. (Yeah, course I'm talking about Home Ec.)

One of the cows had afterbirth left inside her after her calf died. She got all maggoty. Ace had to stick his whole arm up the cow's fanny & leave medicine inside her. Gross.

Hope all is getting better for you. Let me know all about it.

Your bestest
Hannah

Architecture for the lonely, a matching game

Draw a line to match the architecture with the lonely

Empty tin can   Alienate

Cave   XXXX

Tug boat   Slipping under

Basement   Jumping

Rickety bridge   Burying

Floorboards

An opera

Home   Numb

School bus   Turing

Sanatorium   Drowning

Church   Kicking

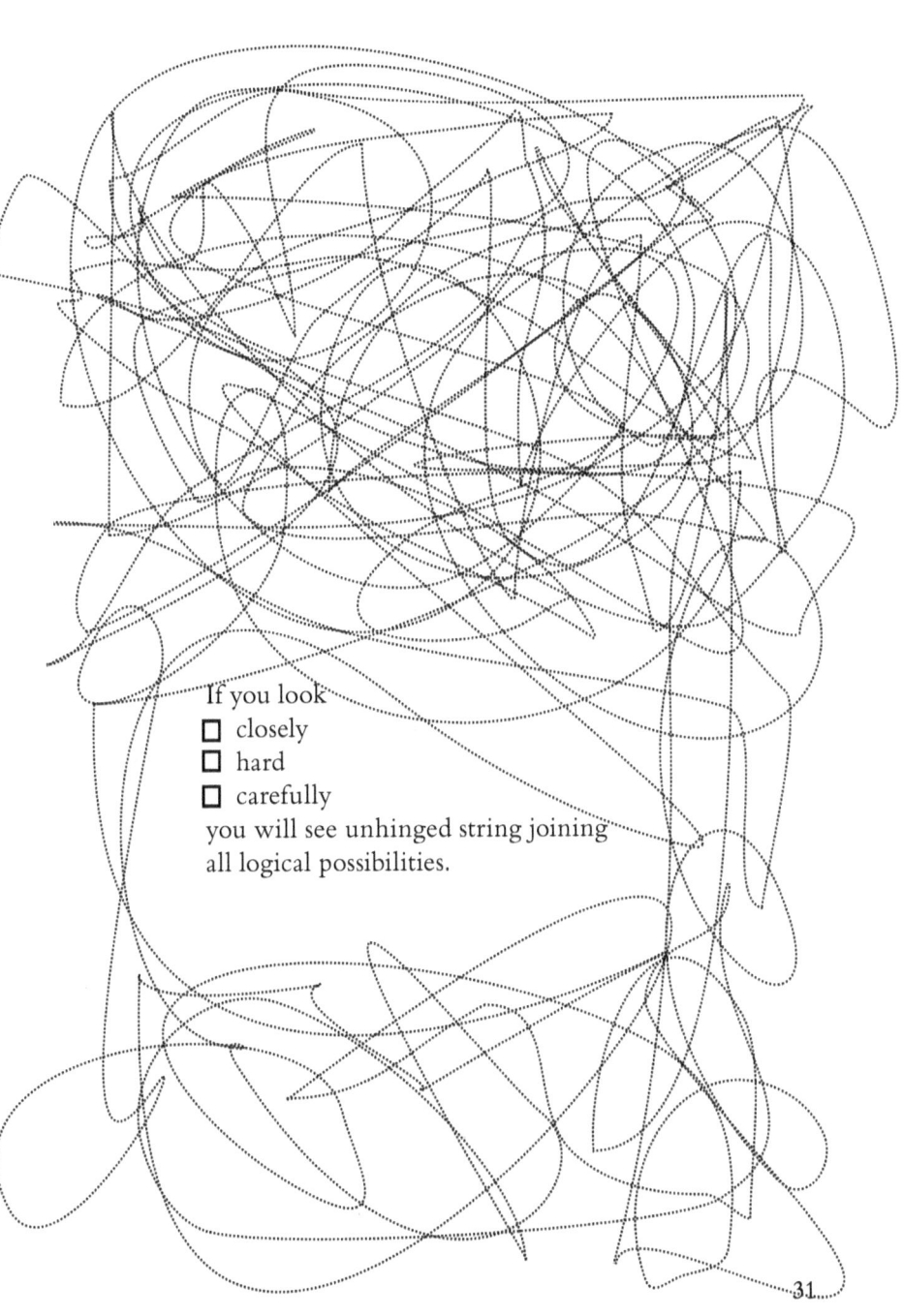

If you look
- ☐ closely
- ☐ hard
- ☐ carefully

you will see unhinged string joining all logical possibilities.

Hugo!

Hey Hu – I'm bursting.

The kids saw me in bed fucking some bloke from the Station & now I am on a total alcohol prohibition. Time to quit & shove it.

Ah, that feels better.

Anyway, who needs a crap job? So, Perth, Port Hedland and Broome should be great. I've always wanted to see WA.

Fuck on.

Love
Hannah

A

My

Your

The

        me

        moat

        blind

                goes

                is

                went

                        mad

                        bonkers

                        bananas

                        nuts

                        crackers

                        suffering from paranoia

*as if a destination, such as Hawaii

Hugo!

Sit down for this one.

You know how I've never had an orgasm? Well, I have now had 2 (two) real-life fair dinkum A-rad orgasms. Proud of me?

I snuck Ace into my room. He was stroking my hair & telling me how tops I am. I was mellow and horny. He was kissing me all over, & then he went down on me. On & on. Deeper & deeper. Then I was exploding. Yeah! I felt electric all over.

Work still sucks but now I have ORGASMS—a precious word deserving all capitals!

Love
Hannah

Ooh	Ah	Mmm
Ergf	Oh	Oh
Yes	Yes	Please
Please	God	Yes
Fuck	Yes	

Inside a house in Tasmania, inside the hidden framework that makes the bones for wall, they found a pile of stuffed-in rags.

They removed the rags, discovering they were a convict's uniform—historians wet their panties—cloth so beautifully preserved—what can we learn from this?

- At one point in time there was an unclothed convict in that house
- Nothing stays hidden forever
- We don't often clean the insides of our walls
- Life was hard [corollary, life is hard]
- I wish I was that convict and I were also free

HEY DUDE

Your letter cracked me up.

Please send stamps to a dude in despair.

Last night I went to Glendambo for a total rave. I ignored my booze ban and got pissed. So did Leon, Ace, Brian and even Sonya was tiddly. It was for drought aid; all the Station people were there.

At 10pm they started a game of footy. Every player was pissed and the umpire was pissed. The commentators were pissed and didn't know anything about football. The crowd kept walking through the game. Utes kept doing doughnuts on the field. It was mad.

Ace & I met these blokes who drive zillionaires in a limo around the bush for a living. No licence, mind. We drank all their piss because they thought I would get on with one of them. Ace & me downed buckets of bourbon then nicked off to hold hands for the bonfire (cute eh?). Leon saw and got mega-cut. Ha ha.

In the car on the way home, Ace and I were too drunk to give a shit and we had our hands all over each other. No-one gave a shit, except Leon. Of course. I'm waiting for Sonya's lecture on appropriate behaviour & getting plastered. This lady is worse than You-Know-Who. The Station can get ripped.

I hope you're having a ball with the tragedies of your life in corridors—tell me about it.

Love, your mate
The Han

Only a handful of laws permit the confinement of someone against their will. Even less permit it in the absence of a crime. Only the Lord of Psych may utter the words of commitment.
See diagram 1.

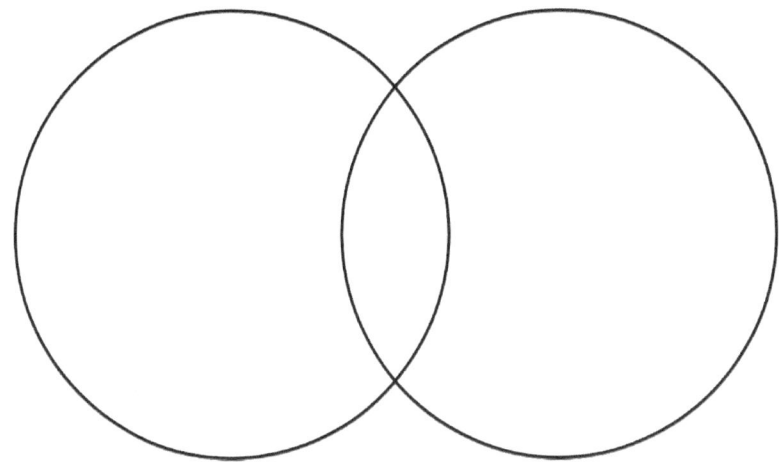

Diagram 1

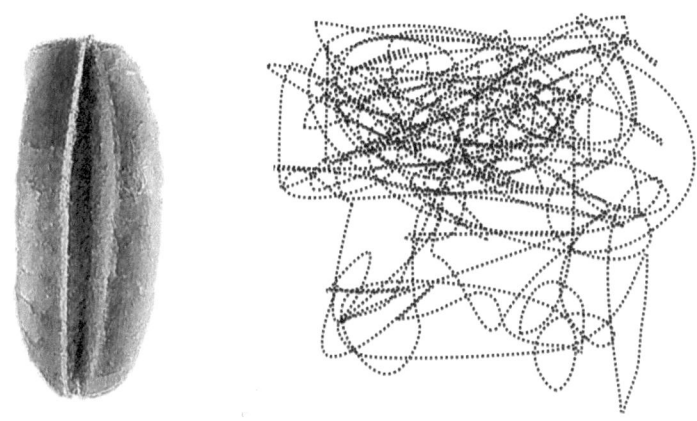

DUDE

I'll be home before Xmas for sure.

Jason sounds like a dream. Tell me the latest—I must know—quickly, quickly.

Mother rang me to plead to go see her. She's told Tom what she did to me. She said it's breaking her heart. I am considering going to see her. She said she'll pay. $$.

It's hard here. I'm under a heap of stress. Stay cool, Han, only 2 weeks to go. I'd leave now except Ace is staying for drenching.

Brian trooped down to my verandah to check if I was drinking. There were 11 empties between me and Ace. (I'd only been drinking ALL day.) What a nerve! Doesn't he trust me or something?

Brian said to Ace that he better not be palming any echoes to "my governess". Ace said, "Not enough". Brian hit the roof and Ace said, "Not palming any cos there's not enough for Hannah as well as me." I nearly died.

I need some marijuana, Hugo. I haven't laughed for a long time. As you can see, I am depressed. Tell me, Hu, have you been sneaking in any smoke on the sly? Is it good?

Thanks for the wish of many orgasms—I've been having heaps. They make life worth living. Sex, and drugs, and rock & roll—the meaning of life.
Oh shut up Hannah you shit-mouthed bitch.

X

I looked you up in DMS.

You were listed on every page.

    That's how much I

        ☐ diagnose

        ☐ love

        ☐ fear

          you.

This book writes itself.

To crack up is not to crack, nor to crack a fat. It is to laugh, heartily.

DUDE

Terrible news.

It is store night and I have just been told there are no smokes. No rollies, paper, baccie—nothing. Can you believe it?!

NO SMOKES—God, I'm going to die. Sonya has probably hidden the cartons. Brian thinks it's piss funny.

Oh Hugo, this Station life is no good at all. And I'm so sick of the food. Hogget and sloppy fucking peas every night. It doesn't even have taste anymore.

Sob ... I want to go home.
H

I TOOK HER ███████, AND I USED ██████.
SHE NEVER SAID YES. I JUST ████████ AND ████████.

I ██████ UNTIL SHE FORGOT HOW TO SAY NO.

HI HUGO

How's life in *Chez Bin*?

You're coming out? I'll come home, home, home & we can go wild.

I just had an A-rad Adelaide weekend. I was meant to go there to sort out my drinking problems. Instead, I had an outrageous time. The food was heaven. Only 7 working days to go in this sinbin.

I finally sent my tax return. Only a month late. And I cancelled my ticket to go see mother. I'm happy about that. She's a simple-minded bitch—even if she does live in Perth. I might forgive her one day, but right now I only have hate.

I read up on Vibratology—the science of vibration, and mystic shit. I am a low vibration person, so I believe in what I want from life and follow it to the end. I find this interesting; am I a nut? It's only as bad as the zodiac.

I'll be back in civilisation soon.

Stay cool, Han.

Love
XO

DEAR HUGO

Not sure I should be writing to you.

I am in a foul mood. I feel like,

1) flattening Brian with his roo-shooting truck

2) hurling the toaster in Sonya's dishwater while she's whinging about lambs

3) roping the kids to be hung, drawn and quartered by their own fucking ponies, and

4) getting so blind drunk and stoned that I throw up all over the mushy peas. Not that it would make any difference, because no-one wants to eat them anyway.

All the staff at the Station are leaving. All of us have quit. Suck that, Sonya, you sloppy pea brain. And Brian you arsehole. I've got 3 days to go, Hugo, & I can't wait another minute.

My crystal mood calendar says I'm on a mood of -10. Who said the occult is bullshit? I will be in the negative till the day I leave. Then it hits +8!

Sorry about this shit of a letter, but I have to tell someone. I need a hard root. I need a big fucking drink. No more letters, Hu, I'm leaving town.

Love always

Han

Q. What is the worst thing you have ever done?

A.

Is there anyone out there
who understands what I mean?

If you understand, fold this page
into a paper plane and fly it to me.

DEAR HUGO

Here is your very late birthday pressie.

I'm sorry that there isn't a card—I can't afford one. I can't even afford smokes. I am broke.

I know you'll like it anyway.

As soon as Xmas is over, I'm saving for Queensland. Things aren't working out with me and Ace.

Better go job hunt.

Write soon.

Hannah

These are just words on a page.

They are not anyone nor anything.

ISOLATING INCIDENT

To isolate, create the conditions in which isolation can sliplessly occur.

When they found out, the knot of the team surrounded me while I sat on the bench. They held me down against the tiled corner of the change room.

Exhibit A.
Bruises at shoulders, thighs and neck. The inside of the mouth does not visibly bruise.

The Captain, ready to shower, stuffed his cock into my mouth. In Court they asked me if he had an erection.

At home, Uncle asked me why I didn't bite. He knows why.

HU!

Thanks for the great news!

Here is some morbid news; I dropped my rod into the murky depths of the mighty Murray. Pissed off man!

Who is this weirdo you are infatuated with? I hope the green trousers you referred to are not 'slacks'. I fucking hate slacks, man. What does he wear them with? Business shirts, Lacoste or billows of patchouli-drenched embroidered cheesecloth? No way, Hugo, this dude gives me bad vibes.

No work. I'll just wait for the picking and harvest to start.

Wolf and I have moved out to a friend's house. I have shelves! No wardrobe though.

I don't think I can see you for a while, as I can't get any work. $$$ are tight. I tried to hide some money but Wolf found it. I am saving to see you when fruit starts. Can't save now but I need $122.00 for my waitressing course.

Hannah

HU

Hi dude

Thanks for your letter. Yes, I had a great new year. Wolf's Dad caught us christening the new pool table. Had to finish off on the kitchen floor. Terrible tile burn—fun.

I'm doing nectarines. Peaches are next. Most nights I pick dried brown goo from my ears and my hair cos we have stone-fruit fights on the floor. I could bake a pie from the dried pulp stuck in my crack. Yuk.

Wolf is easy to live with. I love it.

I can't talk about much else because we work 7 days/week. Only get the day off if it rains.

I had a pipe the other night and got one corner of my mouth drooping. Everyone thought I looked very amusing. I sat there for about 15 mins dribbling and couldn't do a thing about it.

It's a hippy town, this one. Everyone is like a character from a book. Lard is a fat Greek dude. Fred has one leg and can only talk if he's cursing. Pincher drives at 15k/hr cos he's permanently stoned and speed freaks him out. They're all dole-bludging, dope-smoking slobs but kind at heart.

Anyway, I'm doing well. Having lots of fun. Paying back all my debts too.

Lots of love
Han

I like the way you say 'corner'—you push it
from your cakehole like a come on.
It's your flirt word.

DEAR HU

Like, how are you man?

I hope, when you get out, that you are not unemployed like me. I got 9 days fruit work. There are no jobs anywhere. Depressing.

The waitress course will start soon. I'll learn how to serve food & get big tips. I hope so anyway. In the meantime, we go fishing or yabbying for free. We sit in the pub sometimes because it's air-conditioned. Wolf bets on the dogs & he usually wins. We won $150 on Lotto, but all the money goes to the ute.

Poor old Chopper mutt is on 19 pills a day. He only takes them if I crush them into raw liver and kidneys. The pills are working, which is good, cos I don't want him put down.

So, you must write soon. Tell me how your insane life is going & how noisy the rec room is & how cute that male nurse is. Well man, I'll sign off here.

See ya
Han

Five girls took part in a race.

Alison finished before Bunty but behind Clare. Deb finished before Em but behind Bunty.

What was the finishing order?

A.

I fixed him eggs on a good German loaf. He asked, Why the bread?

After breakfast, there was a space where his 'Thank you' should have sat.

I let him in: the fault is mine.

There was another Hugo.
He invented a machine for keeping
the world outside.
In Here is shielded by a flock-lined diving bell.

Deep land diver.

DEAR HUGO

Great news—well for me anyway.

A fortnight off work. Do you know how it feels? Bloody wonderful.

No results from my last biopsy yet. The doctor needs a reading on how bad my warts are before doing the snap-frozen thing (cryotherapy—don't ask). So I wait (& wait, & wait). Wolf and me have got a forest of warts. They spread like fire and burn. All getting me down.

The ute is great though. Of course, for $900 it's got a few probs. Nothing major. In 3 weeks we stick Chopper mutt & all our gear on the back and, you beauty Qld here we come.

I applied for the dole. I could do olives when the other fruit stops but there's not much demand for it. And I'd earn less than the dole because it's a shit job. Fact.

Love ya
Han

PS How is life out & free? Wreaking havoc on the world again?

I am free.

No more staring into the whites of a ram's eye.

I have pills.

I have a hot dog.

HUGO

How are you, dude?

Just thought I'd tell you how much joy I find harvesting. Zilch.

How is your new flat going?

Poor Chopper mutt had to be put down (only after costing $$$, of course). Wolf was so upset he cried heaps but I felt relieved. I reckon he should have been put down ages ago.

Before I got your letter I was feeling guilty about not harvesting. You see, I went out on the farm one day and cut my leg open on a wire fence. It turned septic on me. I can't walk properly yet. All for $19 pay.

The waitressing course fell through. Just excellent. I can see a really bleak future for myself, destined forever to scrounge coins from phone-boxes and parking meters. I won $10 on the ponies today; that's not a bad income, eh? Yes, professional gambling sounds just the thing.

Wolf has been working night shifts. It's a cunt. He sleeps all day & if I accidentally wake him he gives me criminal glares. But, I tell you, when he rocks in at 8am & jumps into bed, he doesn't think twice about switching on the idiot box & waking me up.
Unreal.

Write soon

Han

I gave him a bouquet of carved wooden flowers. He used them as a dildo, rocking himself on the unopened buds while fist-coaxing his cock to come.

I love the flowers, he said, Thank you.

Hey hotdog. I've got your bun.

HUGS

Welcome to Queensland. Beautiful one day, Japanese the next.

Looking for a place, we might sign a lease today for a shitbox near a dairy. Be nice to stop sleeping on the back of the ute. The mossies are a bit much but at least it's warm.

I'll send you my address when it's fixed.

Surely
Han

DEAR HUGO

The mill has been going for a couple of days now.

—the smoke makes you feel gross—it stinks. Babinda is pretty except for the foul mill-spew.

The other weekend I went to el-Arish. I saw a duck, an Irish setter, a turkey and a little old woman walking in a line down the main street. There was a mob of pigeons in the street too, getting in the way of all the cars. When the train goes through, the driver chucks out bread crumbs & the street swells with pigeons. Weird man.

Getting my warts treated soon—expensive. I'm shit-scared too. The doctor wants me to go private so I can have a new fabbo laser therapy because my warts are so big and so many. Least I know there is one thing I can do: breed cauliflower warts like there's no tomorrow.

Oh well, rid of them altogether, eventually.

Love
Han

You pull the wooden flower, warm, from inside me.

When did that happen? I don't remember.

If you want to not be predictable, what are you?

(Clue: the answer is not UN-pre...).

Dear Hugo

I have not had a good root lately.

I just had my warts lasered off my poor little fanny and am a bit sore. They'd spread to my arse so I had my rectum lasered too. Not allowed to root for 4 weeks. The doctor said I will get more warts because I was very infected. He also said I will be in pain for some time as I have a lot of lacerated tissue.

(Lacerated, what a mean word.)

Not to worry—I can relax in a shallow antiseptic bath (ye-ow).

I am enjoying work, but a new girl is starting who is 17 yo. So, all our hours will be given to her because she is cheaper. Doesn't that suck? How is your new job going?

I found a wardrobe at the tip but I will have to leave it behind when we move again. We have no idea where we are going next.

I watched the sugarcane on fire. They burnt that shit to the ground.

Well, please write soon.
Han

Did you have to make it genital warts?
And
did you have to have so very many?

Where do you go when you're not here, he asked me.

I go to me, I said.

He traced his fingertip around my lip line and said, I want to go there too.

Who talks from the gutter?

rats witches snakes fallen leaves dust hubcaps horse-shit

HUGO!

Hiya! Long time, no see.

Things are going good up here in Port Douglas—still no car though. The weather is just magnificent—at night you can go out with just a T-shirt on and not be cold. I have been in Port D. for nine months—in the one town!

I have started a wrestling class which is great fun. I had to 'grapple' a spunky young thing into my chest yesterday. It was jolly good fun—he blushed for thirty minutes. I'm the only woman in the class. Jake, my lover de jour, is not impressed. The poor lamb.

Jake worries me—what am I doing with this piece of meat? If people see me alone they ask where he is. I tell them 'he's naked in my bed, where he belongs'. I'm such a crack-up, eh?

I've got warts in my throat. I thought I had a flu but its turns out not being able to swallow was due to the wart plantation filling my oesophagus.

There's a heap of luxury apartments being built next to my caravan—the entire place is crawling with spunky workmen. It's great! My favourite is this little one who wears short shorts and climbs tall ladders. I don't know who he is so I've named him Sparky and given him my 'Best Arse in Town' personal achievement award. He can come and pick it up en-ee-time, mate.

You must forgive me, I am going through a disturbing sex maniac phase. I should grow out of it.

Hooroo
Han

Come to bed. I need you to suck me off, he said.

I followed to avoid a fight.

While he slept I lay strands of cotton across his throat.

It's not abuse if you don't say no.

I need you to penetrate me more, he said. Not more often, more spiritually. I need to feel you worship at the altar of my anus.

I opened the oven to check the bubbling enchiladas.

It looked quiet inside.

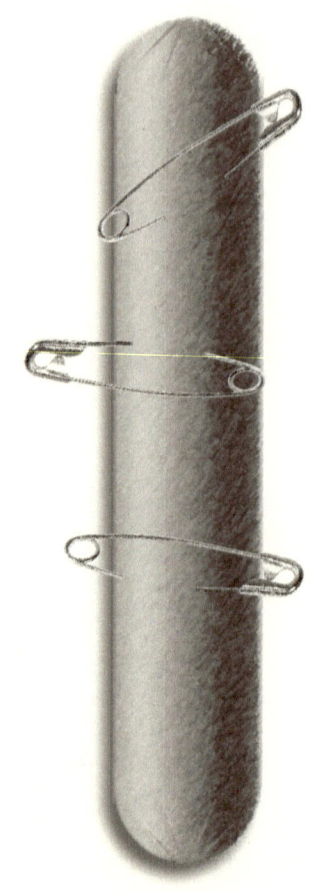

Afterword

What is it to be isolated?

A while ago, when I shared an office space with two busy, extroverted colleagues, Adam Dickerson delighted me with a copy of a photograph showing a hard-at-work desk-bound person wearing an invention from 1925 called The Isolator. The Isolator's creator, Hugo Gernsback, was a member of the American Physical Society, and publisher of scientifiction.

The Isolator is an oversized dome-shaped, full-head helmet. A tube connects the Isolator to a portable oxygen tank while two horizontal slits in round eye windows provide a restricted visual focus. The image caption describes the helmet thus; 'The author at work in his private study aided by the Isolator. Outside noises being eliminated, the worker can concentrate with ease upon the subject at hand.'

It could be argued that Hugo Gernsback's invention goes too far in pursuit of productive solitude. I have tried to follow him here, in this work, by going too far for then nothing remains for regret.

Acknowledgements

This book was made possible by the inspiration and support of Recent Work Press, especially chief creator and comrade Shane Strange who encourages such contributions to the Mehrprodukt and decadence shaping our age, and Silvana Moro who assisted with editing and layout.

Drawings on pages 9, 28 and 34 are extracts from illustrations in Alexandre Dumas' The Count of Monte-Cristo (1888, London: George Routledge).

Monica Carroll writes and performs short and short-ish creative and experimental works. She likes to mix poetry, paper and embroidery. She holds a PhD in philosophy and poetry. Her current interests include artists' books, phenomenology, space and empathy.

www.monicacarroll.com.au

2016 Editions

Pulse **Prose Poetry Project**
Incantations **Subhash Jaireth**
Transit **Niloofar Fanaiyan**
Gallery of Antique Art **Paul Hetherington**
Sentences from the Archive **Jen Webb**
River's Edge **Owen Bullock**

2017 Editions

A Song, the World to Come **Miranda Lello**
Cities: Ten Poets, Ten Cities **Various**
The Bulmer Murder **Paul Munden**
Dew and Broken Glass **Penny Drysdale**
Members Only **Melinda Smith** and **Caren Florance**
the future, un-imagine **Angela Gardner** and **Caren Florance**
Proof **Maggie Shapley**
Black Tulips **Moya Pacey**
Soap **Charlotte Guest**
Isolator **Monica Carroll**
Ikaros **Paul Hetherington**
Work & Play **Owen Bullock**

all titles available from
www.recentworkpress.com

www.ingramcontent.com/pod-product-compliance
Lightning Source LLC
Chambersburg PA
CBHW032048290426
44110CB00012B/1005